A CLOAK FOR THE DREAMER

For Aunty Ann, who sent us all off into the world but still looks after us. —A.F.

For Molly, Levi, and Jacob Larkey. —K.H.

Copyright © 1994 by Marilyn Burns Education Associates
All rights reserved. Published by Scholastic Inc.

Marilyn Burns Brainy Day Books is a trademark of Marilyn Burns Education Associates.

25 24 23   05

Printed in Singapore   46

The illustrations in this book were done with pencil and watercolors on 300 lb. watercolor paper.

Library of Congress Cataloging-in-Publication Data

Friedman, Aileen
    A cloak for the dreamer / by Aileen Friedman; illustrated by Kim Howard.
        p.   cm.
    "A Marilyn Burns brainy day book."
    Summary: When a tailor asks each of his three sons to make a cloak for the archduke, the third son's design reveals his desire to travel the world rather than follow in his father's footsteps.
    ISBN 0-590-48987-9
    [1. Tailors—Fiction.   2. Individuality—Fiction.   3. Fathers and sons—Fiction.]   I. Howard, Kim, ill.   II. Title.
PZ7.F8964C1   1994
[E]—dc20   94-11274
                                                                    CIP
                                                                    AC

A CLOAK FOR THE DREAMER

written by AILEEN FRIEDMAN ❖ illustrated by KIM HOWARD

A Marilyn Burns Brainy Day Book

SCHOLASTIC INC. ❖ NEW YORK

Once there was a tailor who had three fine sons. The tailor loved his sons and appreciated their helpfulness.

Ivan, the oldest son, picked up all the pins from the floor of his father's shop and gathered together all the little pieces of loose thread. Whenever he could, Ivan watched his father measure, cut, and sew. He wanted to be a tailor himself one day and work alongside his father.

Alex, the middle son, brought his father bolts of fabric to cut and then carefully put them away. Whenever he could, Alex practiced sewing together the small, leftover pieces of fabric. He, too, wanted to be a tailor and work alongside his father.

Misha, the youngest son, carried the finished jackets and cloaks and dresses to his father's customers all over town. Whenever he could, he stopped at the bookseller's shop around the corner. There, he pored over maps of the world and pictures of faraway places. Unlike his brothers, Misha did not want to be a tailor and work alongside his father. He dreamed instead of traveling far and wide, and of making his own way in the world.

One morning, the tailor gathered his three sons before him. "Now is the time," he said, "for each of you to show that you can do the work of a tailor.

"Our good customer, the Archduke, leaves on an important journey in just three days. For this journey, he has ordered three new cloaks for himself and three dresses for his wife. I can sew the dresses, but, to get the job done on time, each of you must make one cloak."

The sons were glad to help their father and listened carefully to his instructions.

"First of all," explained the tailor, "the Archduke wants his cloaks to be very colorful. Every bolt of fabric we have is of just one color, so each of you will have to cut pieces from many bolts and sew them into a single colorful cloth of your own design. Of course, the cloak you fashion from your cloth will also have to protect the Archduke from the wind and the rain. Work by yourselves, so that all three cloaks will be different."

The sons got busy right away.

Ivan first studied the bolts of fabric. He had seen his father use them all at one time or another, so he cut a rectangle from each one. Then, using the pattern of bricks on the floor, Ivan carefully sewed the rectangles together. From this beautiful cloth of many colors, he fashioned a cloak for the Archduke. Ivan was ready on the morning of the third day to present the cloak to his father.

Meanwhile, Alex had thought of the colors of the Archduke's carriage and the coat of arms that was painted on its side. He pulled down the bolts of red, yellow, and purple fabric and cut many squares from each bolt. He nimbly stitched the squares together to make one beautiful cloth of the Archduke's colors, then fashioned the cloth into a sturdy cloak. Because of all his sewing practice, Alex worked quickly enough to have his cloak ready by the morning of the second day.

With a day to spare, Alex had time to worry. "Perhaps my cloak isn't interesting enough," he thought. "Perhaps the Archduke would want something more." He thought again of the Archduke's coat of arms and the pattern of its background. Then he went back to work.

Alex cut more red, yellow, and purple squares, but this time he snipped them in half on the diagonal. He sewed these triangles together to match the pattern on the Archduke's coat of arms, and fashioned this new cloth into another cloak. Alex sewed even faster than he had the first time, and the second cloak was ready on the morning of the third day.

All the while, Misha was working, too. He thought of going out into the world as he cut circles from the bolts of fabric. He picked his colors from the maps he loved — blue for the deep oceans and winding rivers, green for the meadows of the countryside, yellow for the sands of the deserts, red for the routes between faraway places.

Misha sewed his circles together, carefully joining them where they met, and the cloth he made was beautiful. But when he held it up to the light, Misha saw that it was full of open spaces. He could tell this cloth wouldn't make a proper cloak, but he did not have time to start over. Although he worried that the cloak would disappoint his father, Misha completed it in time.

On the morning of the third day, when the tailor had sewn the last stitch on the third dress for the Archduke's wife, he called for his sons to bring in their cloaks.

Ivan proudly showed his cloak of many-colored rectangles.

"You have made a beautiful cloak, Ivan," said the tailor. "I am honored to present it to the Archduke. From now on, you will be a tailor, too, and work alongside your father."

Happy for his brother, but still unsure of his own work, Alex
showed his two cloaks to his father.

"Why, Alex," said the tailor, "you have made *two* beautiful
cloaks! How thoughtful of you to use the Archduke's own colors.
He will be thrilled to wear these, I'm sure. And your quick, even
stitches show me that you, too, are ready to be a tailor and work
alongside your father."

"I see your dreams of traveling the world in all the circles of your cloak," continued the tailor. "Do you think it is time for you to cross these oceans and rivers, meadows and deserts, and to follow these routes to faraway places?"

"Yes, Father," answered Misha.

"Then take these cloaks and dresses to the Archduke, and come back to get ready for your own journey. Tomorrow your brothers and I will send you off into the world."

That night the tailor sat in his little shop, looking sadly at his third son's beautiful, but useless, cloak. Though he knew Misha had to leave home, he hated to see him go. He knew Ivan and Alex felt just as bad as he did.

"If only we could give Misha something to protect him as he makes his own way in the world," the tailor thought. He sat by the fire a little longer, and then he had an idea.

The tailor ran up the stairs and quietly woke Ivan and Alex.
"I know what we can give Misha to take on his journey into the world," whispered the tailor. "We can make him a new cloak from his own cloak of circles. That way, it will have all the colors of his dreams, but it will be sewn together in the practical way tailors sew things — and it will protect him from the wind and the rain."

"But how, Father?" asked Ivan. "The circles won't fit together."

"I know, my son," said the tailor. He motioned for his sons to follow him downstairs to the shop. There he explained how it could be done.

All night long the tailor and his two oldest sons worked on Misha's cloak. Ivan snipped the circles apart, and his father trimmed them into hexagons. As his father cut, Alex quickly sewed the hexagons together to make one cloth of the dreamer's colors. When the cloth was finished, the three tailors fashioned it into a strong and beautiful cloak. They stitched the last stitch as the sun came up on the day Misha was to leave home.

Later that morning, the tailor and his sons
Ivan and Alex kissed and hugged Misha good-bye
at the door of their little shop. Then they stood
together and watched as the dreamer set off into
the world, his beautiful cloak growing smaller
and smaller in the distance.

For Parents, Teachers, and Other Adults

Although it's obvious to adults that circles sewn together will produce a cloth full of holes, while squares and rectangles nestle together snugly, it may not be obvious to children. Children's understanding of geometric concepts depends on their age, the particular experiences they've had exploring shapes, and the thinking they've done about relationships among shapes. *A Cloak for the Dreamer* contributes to children's geometric learning by presenting them with a context for thinking about geometric shapes and how they can fit together.

About the Mathematics

Whether or not shapes fit together has to do with their angles. Squares and rectangles have right angles, each 90 degrees. You can place four right angles (360 degrees altogether) to surround a point completely and leave no holes. These numbers—90 degrees in a square corner and 360 degrees for a full rotation — are arbitrary measures. But since they are agreed-upon mathematical conventions, we accept them and use them when communicating about angles.

In the story, all of the triangles Alex used were cut on the diagonal from squares. They are called isosceles right triangles, "isosceles" because they have two sides the same length and "right" because they have a square corner, a 90-degree right angle. The other two angles are halves of right angles and, therefore, measure 45 degrees each. Because there are several combinations of 90 and 45 that add up exactly to 360, it's possible to fit together isosceles right triangles in different ways.

But how about piecing together equilateral triangles? Or isosceles triangles without 90-degree angles? Or scalene triangles? And what about quadrilaterals (four-sided shapes) other than squares or rectangles?

| equilateral triangle | isosceles right triangle | parallelogram | rhombus | scalene triangle |

It turns out that it's possible to piece any triangle or quadrilateral into a patchwork design. That's because the sum of the four interior angles of quadrilaterals equals 360 degrees, just enough to fill the space around a point. The sum of the three interior angles of triangles equals 180 degrees and, therefore, the angles of two triangles add up to 360 degrees. (You may need to cut and piece shapes to convince yourself. There's often no substitute for using physical materials to prove a theory.)

The problem with circles is that they don't have angles, so there's no way to wedge them into tight fits.

But why did the hexagons work? Again, it has to do with the angles. The sum of the interior angles of a hexagon is 720 degrees. This fact makes sense if you agree that a triangle has 180 degrees and you see how hexagons can be partitioned into four triangles

(4 × 180 = 720). Regular hexagons, like the ones the tailor cut, have six angles the same size, each 120 degrees (720 ÷ 6). And since three 120's make 360, regular hexagons can be pieced together into a cloth.

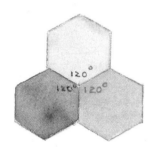

Most likely the tailor didn't do this kind of formal mathematical thinking before cutting the circles into hexagons. Maybe he'd seen a floor tiled in hexagons. Or perhaps he knew they would work just as they do in beehives, where all the cells are hexagons. Much of our geometric learning comes from observing the world around us.

Not all polygons fit together this way. For example, regular octagons, when used for floor tiles, are usually paired with squares. That's because each angle of a regular octagon measures 135 degrees and 135 + 135 + 90 = 360. There's no way to get exactly 360 degrees with only 135-degree angles.

Back to the children. Young children don't have the developmental maturity or geometric experience necessary to understand the formal mathematics of fitting shapes together. But their beginning explorations with shapes can provide a useful foundation for their later, more formal study of geometry. And with sufficient opportunities to explore geometric ideas, children can develop a curiosity about shapes and the confidence to pursue new ideas.

Extending Children's Learning

To encourage and extend children's thinking after reading the story, engage them in the following:

1. Look at fabrics on clothing and upholstery and identify the different shapes used.

2. Look for shapes elsewhere in the world—in the house, in the supermarket, on walks, while driving in the car.

3. If you have any patchwork quilts or pillows, examine their patterns. Or look for examples of patchwork in stores, magazines, and books. Talk about the shapes used in the designs.

4. Give children construction paper, scissors, and glue and have them choose one shape from the book (square, rectangle, triangle, or hexagon), cut the shape out of different colors of paper, and create patterns by fitting them together.

5. Suggest that children create patterns using more than one shape. Can squares and rectangles be pieced together to make a cloth? What about squares and triangles? Or rectangles and triangles? What about squares or rectangles of different sizes in one pattern? Will hexagons work with other shapes?

While there is mathematical content in *A Cloak for the Dreamer,* keep in mind that the book is meant to engage and delight children, stimulate their imaginations, and encourage them to develop a love of books and reading. As with any book, invite children's reactions. Some children may interrupt the story to express an idea or ask a question. Some may want to talk about the illustrations. Others may listen intently until the end. All of these reactions are fine. At all times, follow the child's lead.